Mel Bay Presents

EZ Way to Tune Guitars

By Roger Filiberto

I0808392

Visit us on the Web at www.melbay.com — E-mail us at email@melbay.com

PREFACE

"How to tune the Guitar" is for every one who plays the guitar...the beginner, the advanced, the professional.

For the beginner, two Major Systems of tuning, to which the greater part of this instruction book is dedicated, and for the advanced and the professional, a good many ideas for the development of "pin point" tuning.

The two Major Systems teach the beginner to tune from a "reference string".*

System Number One teaches the beginner to tune from the 6th or "E" string (the reference string) to the 1st string which is also an "E" string but which is two octaves up from the 6th.

System Number Two begins with the 1st string (reference string) and works downward to the 6th string.

The last portion of this book, from page 17 to the end, is for the advanced guitarist and the professional.

There are many ways to tune a guitar,...which eventually, with time and experience, the guitarist will discover. However, most players tune their instrument the basic way, beginning with the "reference string."

There is NO substitute for the basic or fundamental way. Tuning System Number One and System Number Two are BASIC and FUNDAMENTAL.

EDITOR'S NOTE:

***The "reference string" is the one you tune to the Piano, Pitch-pipe or Tuning Fork. In other words, the "starting" string.**

THE GUITAR NECK

The Names of the Strings

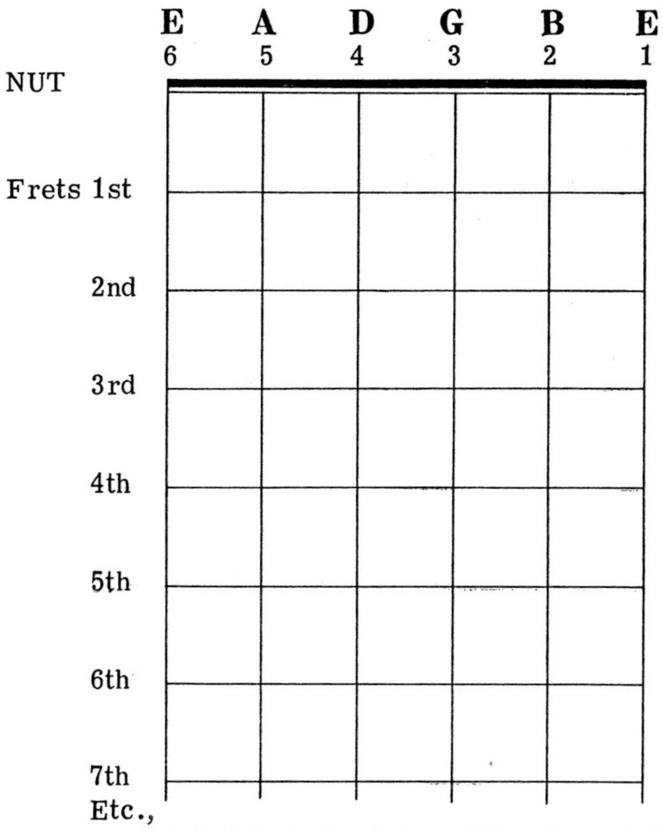

The First string is the thinnest string.

The Sixth string is the thickest string.

This page is just to acquaint you with the open strings of the guitar and their relationship to the piano keyboard.

We do not recommend the use of this page to tune the guitar until you have completed Tuning System Number One.

Comprehensive tuning lessons begin on page four.

Below is a chart describing the relationship of the sound (pitch) of the open guitar strings to the piano keyboard.

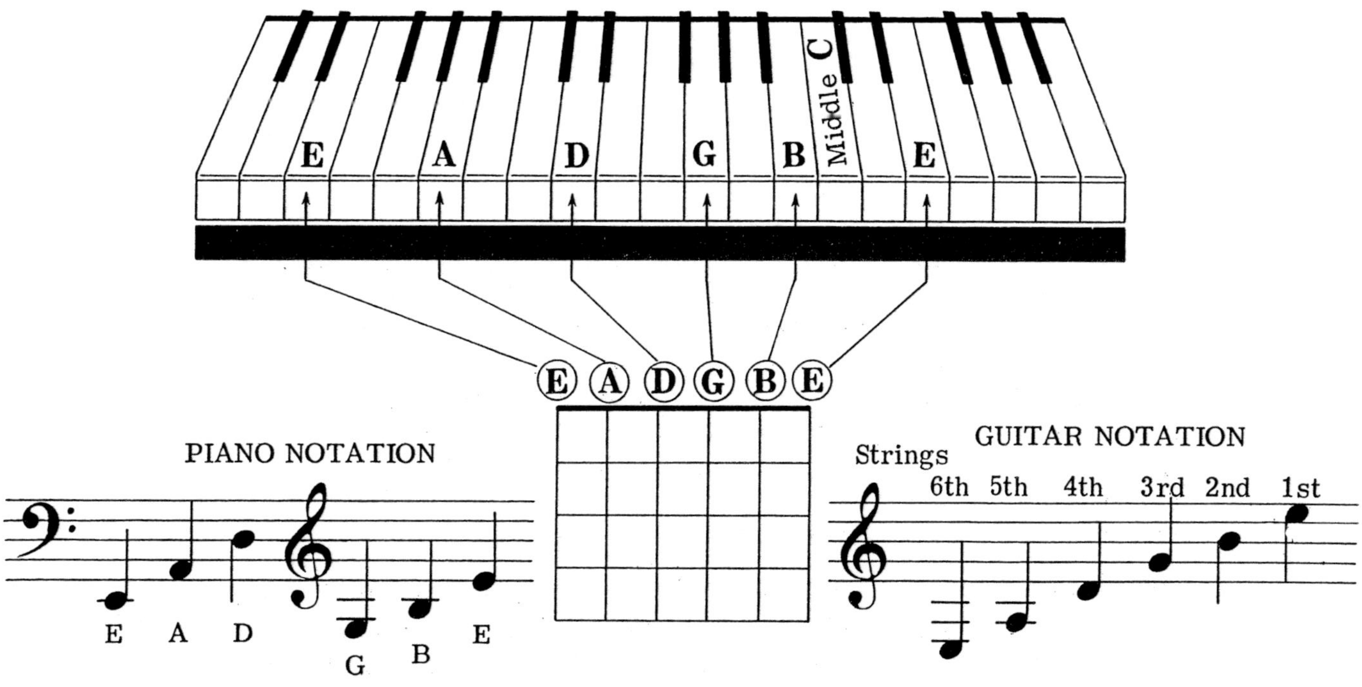

TUNING SYSTEM NUMBER ONE
LESSON NUMBER ONE
Tuning the "E" or Sixth String

Tuning your guitar starting from the big "E" or 6th string is probably the most widely used and accepted method of tuning.

If you have a piano or have access to one, tune the 6th string so that it will sound the same as the E or twelfth white key to the LEFT of middle C on the piano. You will find a comprehensive chart of the piano keyboard showing Middle C on page three.

> If a piano is not available use the pitch-pipe low "E" (6th) string tone. See foot-note*.

Below is a chart or diagram of the guitar neck showing the "E" open 6th string and the Guitar and Piano notation of the "E" sound on the music staff.

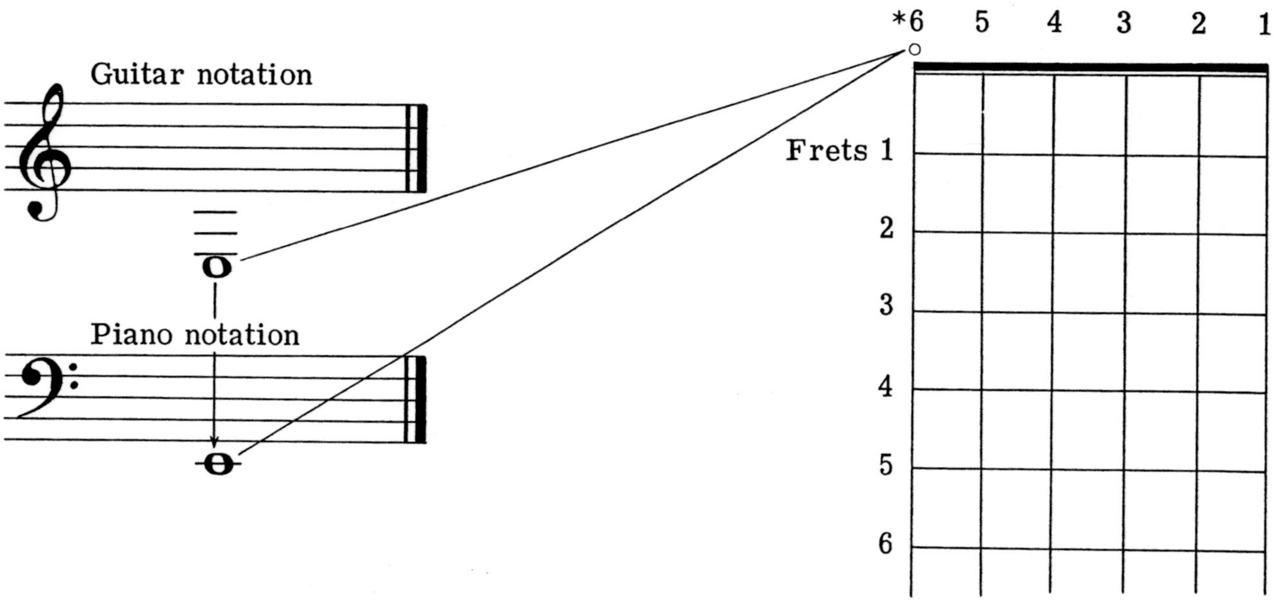

* The reference string.

It is easier to tune a string by tightening it, so, begin by loosening or unwinding the string you are about to tune. By so doing you know that you must <u>TIGHTEN</u> the string to reach the necessary tone (pitch) which in this case is obtained from the piano or pitch-pipe. Tune slowly at first, checking many times until you reach the proper tone (pitch). It is more than likely that your first attempts will be unsuccessful. However don't get discouraged as persistence and determination will inevitably bring success.

> * Pitch-pipes
>
> Pitch-pipes with instructions for their usage may be obtained at any music store or guitar studio. Each pipe will have the correct pitch of each guitar string and the use of the pitch-pipe is recommended when a piano is not available.

LESSON NUMBER TWO

Tuning the "A" or 5th String

To tune the 5th string, place a finger of the left hand on the 5th fret of the "E" or 6th string. This note, on the 6th string is the same "A" note as the open "A" or 5th string.

Below, at the right, is a diagram of the two identical Guitar "A" notes, and on the left, the guitar and piano notation of the identical "A" sound on the music staff.

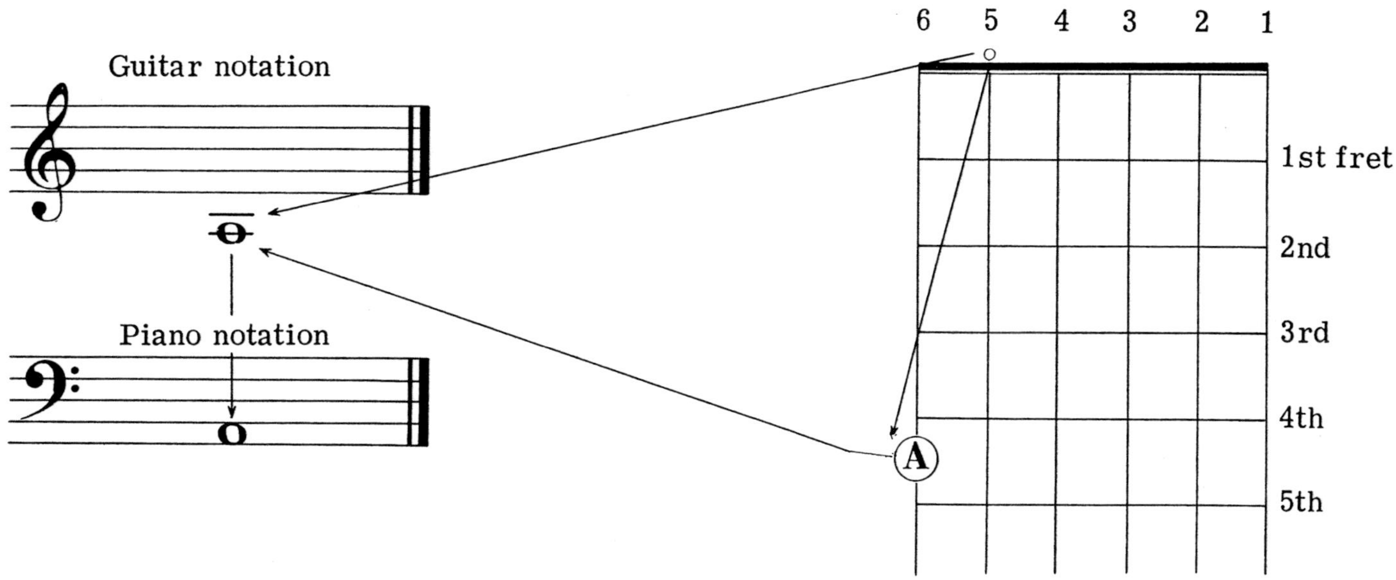

The first step toward tuning the Fifth string is to <u>LOOSEN</u> this string thereby making it necessary to tighten it in order to match the tone or pitch of the 5th fret of the 6th string. This process is called "raising" the pitch. Work slowly, checking the two tones often and when you feel that you are "close" or in tune, strike the two strings simultaneously, and if you are "in tune" the two strings will sound as one tone, without discord or conflict.

Practice tuning the 6th and 5th strings many times before proceeding to the 4th string. Try to accept the fact that tuning is a slow process and it will be some time before you can come up with a perfect tuning job. You will improve with time. Some days you do better than on other days. This is the way it is. The more practice you get the more you improve.

LESSON NUMBER THREE
Tuning the "D" or 4th String

To tune the 4th string, place a finger of the left hand on the 5th fret of the "A" or 5th string. This note, (on the 5th string) is the same "D" note as the open 4th string.

Below, at the right, is a diagram of the two indentical Guitar "D" notes, and on the left, the guitar and piano notation of the identical "D" sound on the music staff.

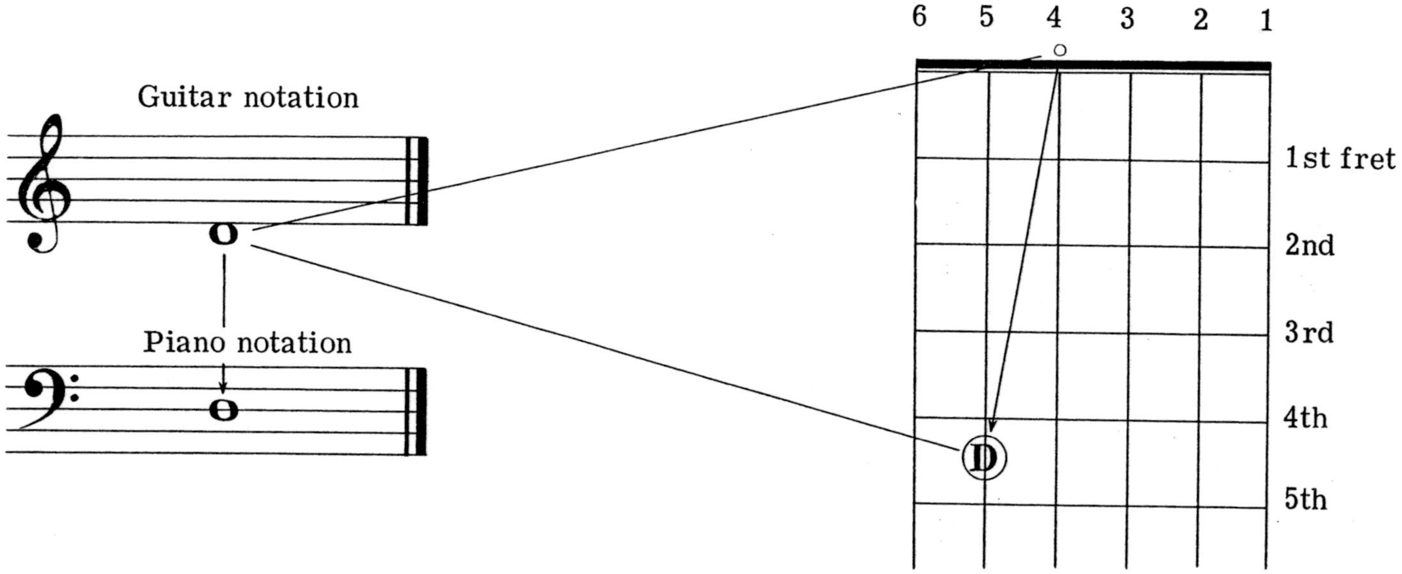

Follow the same procedure as in the previous lessons. LOOSEN the 4th string, then begin tightening it until the tone or pitch sounds the same as the 5th fret of the 5th string. As in the previous lessons, work slowly, checking the two tones often. The most frequent and common mistake of the beginner is TIGHTENING the string too much thus going higher than the necessary pitch. If you are in doubt and feel that you may possibly have tightened the string too much, loosen the string and start all over again. If you are taking lessons your teacher will guide you properly.

At this stage you should be reviewing all previous tuning lessons and satisfy yourself that you are making progress before proceeding to the next string.

Follow this four point doctrine.

1. Persistence
2. Determination
3. Perseverance
4. Tenacity

LESSON NUMBER FOUR

Tuning the "G" or 3rd String

To tune the 3rd string, place a finger of the left hand on the 5th fret of the "D" or 4th string. This note, on the 4th string is the same "G" note as the open 3rd string.

Below, at the right, is a diagram of the two identical Guitar "G" notes, and on the left, the guitar and piano notation of the identical "G" sound on the music staff.

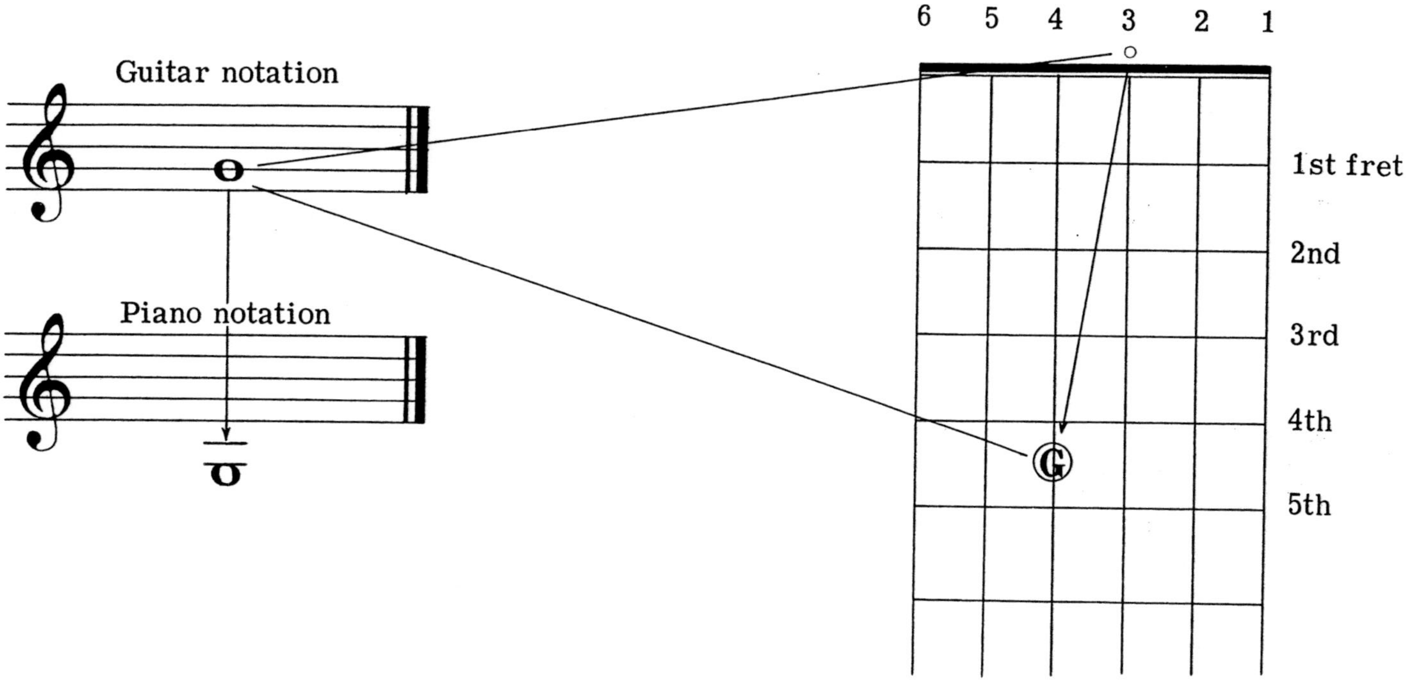

Continue in the same manner as in the previous lessons. Loosen the "G" (3rd) string so that is will be necessary to tighten this string so as to match the tone or pitch of the 5th fret of the "D" or 4th string. Follow all previous rules and instructions.

At this point the ear training that you have been acquiring is going to be a big help to you in recognizing the identical sounds.

LESSON NUMBER FIVE

Tuning the "B" or 2nd String

To tune the 2nd string, place a finger of the left hand on the 4th fret of the "G" or 3rd string. This note, on the 3rd string is the same "B" note as the open 2nd string.

Below, at the right, is a diagram of the two identical Guitar "B" notes, and on the left, the guitar and piano notation of the identical "B" sound on the music staff.

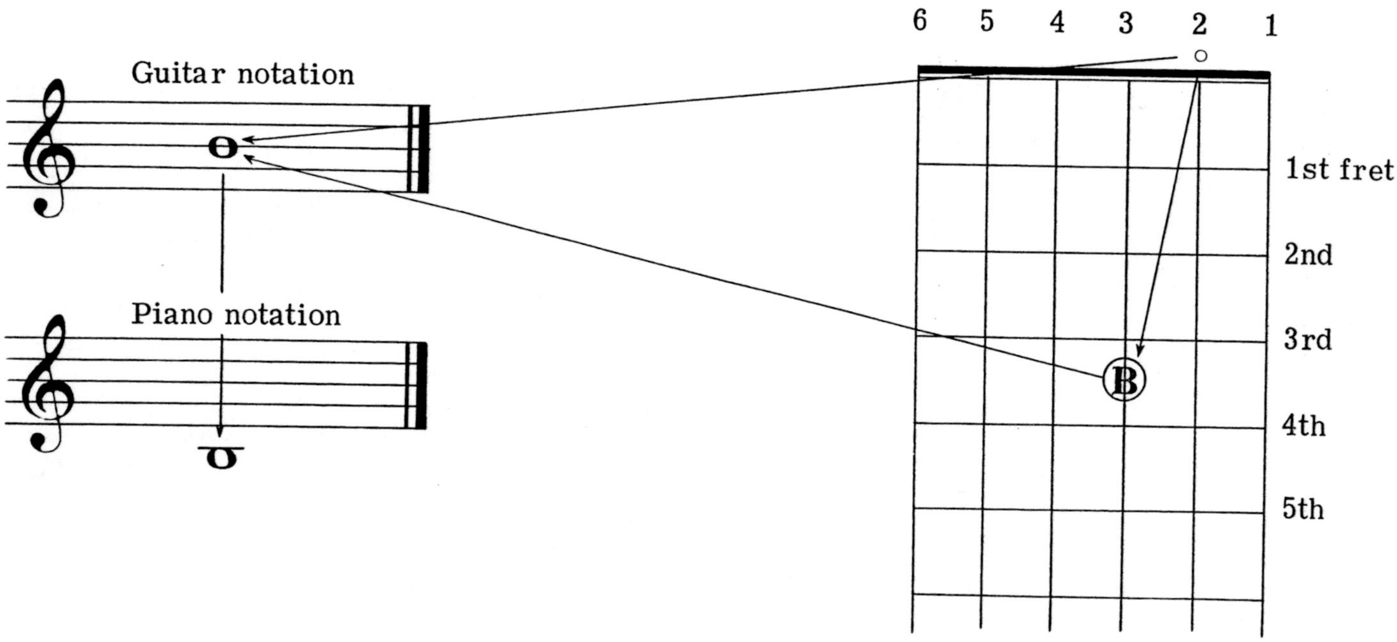

Procedures and instructions are the same as in all previous lessons.

Keep the following four points in mind:

1. Loosen the string you are tuning.
2. Hold the 3rd string down at the 4th fret.
3. Tighten the open 2nd string so that it will match the tone of the 4th fret of the 3rd string.
4. Tune slowly. Never hurry.

LESSON NUMBER SIX

Tuning the "E" or 1st String

To tune the 1st string, place a finger of the left hand on the 5th fret of the "B" or 2nd string. This note, on the 2nd string is the same "E" note as the open 1st string.

Below, at the right, is a diagram of the two identical Guitar "E" notes, and on the left, the guitar and piano notation of the identical "E" sound on the music staff.

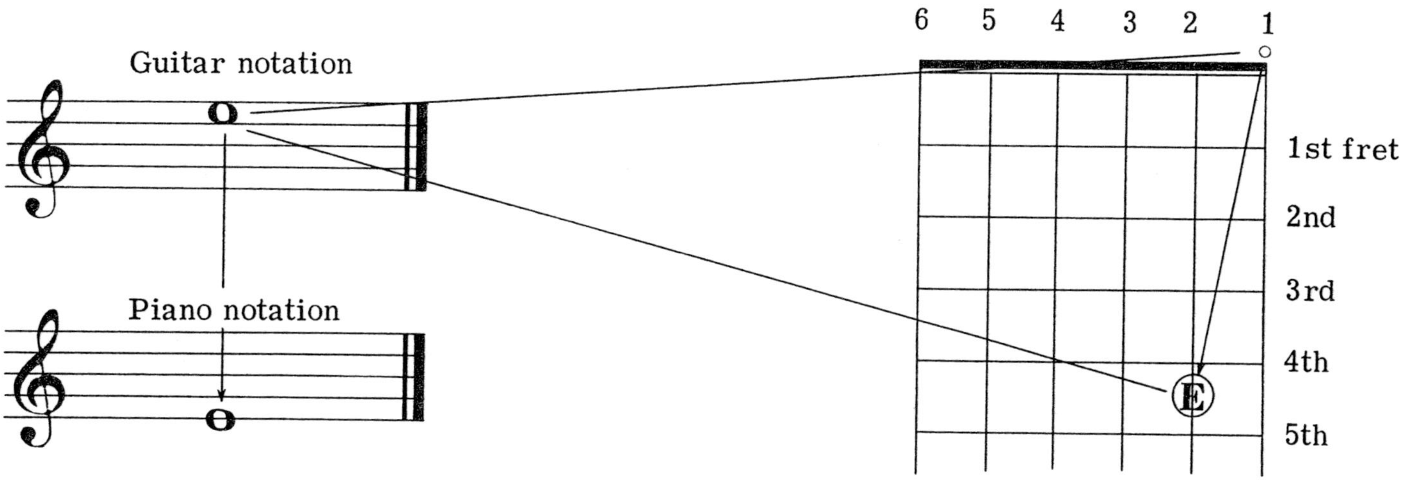

Rules and procedures are obviously unnecessary at this point. If you have followed all instructions faithfully you are now ready for the final touch up.

THE IMPORTANT FINAL STEP
The final "touch-up".

Having completed the tuning cycle, re-check all strings in the order in which you tuned them. Do this at least twice.

THE REASON FOR THIS

As you adjust each string to it's required pitch the tension on the bridge and "top" of the guitar changes with the tuning of each string. When you have reached the final step of the tuning cycle, all of the strings, including the "reference string" will be slightly "off" pitch thus making it necessary to adjust each string a little bit in order to make your final "touch up" perfect. CHECK PAGE FOUR FOR REFERENCE STRING.

At this point you can use the Piano Keyboard on page three, tuning each string to the identical note on the Keyboard.
You can also use the complete 6 string Pitch Pipe, tuning each string to the identical sound on the Pipe.

TUNING SYSTEM NUMBER TWO
LESSON NUMBER ONE
Tuning the First or "E" String

The first step is to get an "A" 440 tuning fork or an "A" 440 pitch pipe. Any brand will do as most manufacturers make a decent product. Then, place any finger of the left hand on the 5th fret of this string and match the sound or pitch of the tuning fork or the pitch pipe "A". Before proceeding read detailed instructions at bottom of page.*

Below is a diagram of the guitar neck showing the "A" at the 5th fret and the Guitar notation of the identical sound on the music staff.

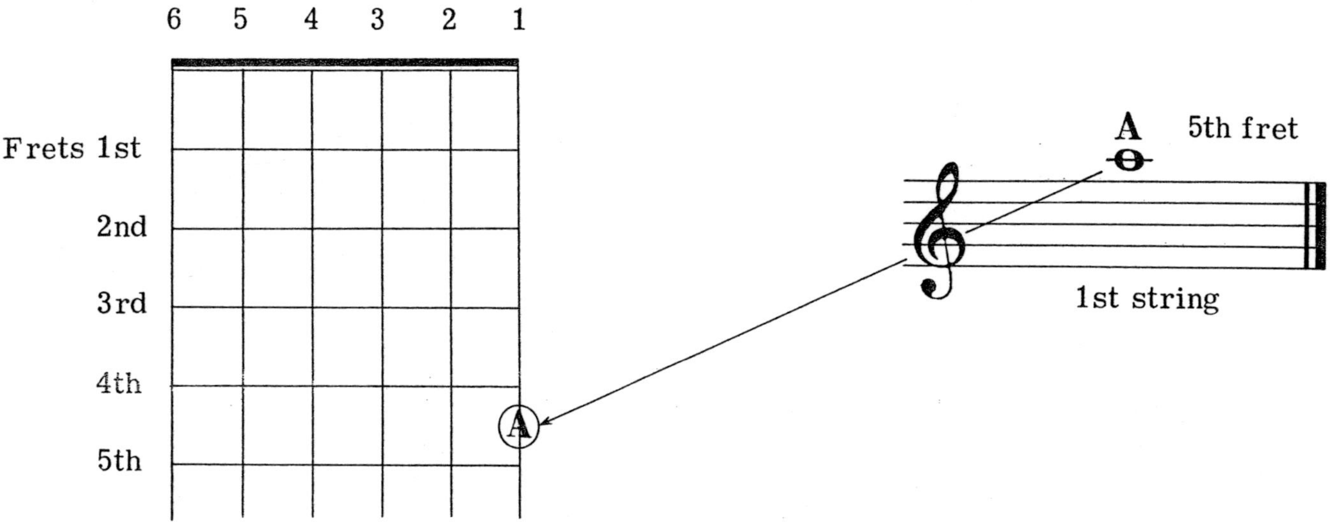

*When tuning to reach the required tone or pitch it is best to do so by tightening the string. Therefore, your first step will be to loosen the string so that it will be lower than the required pitch, thus making it necessary to tighten it in order to reach the correct tone. Do this slowly at first, checking frequently until you reach the "A" 440 of the pitch pipe or the tuning fork. This will be a slow process and you may not be completely successful in the first few attempts. Persistence and perseverance will eventually bring success.

When you have successfully tuned your first string to the "A" sound or pitch this will mean that your open "E" or 1st string is in tune. For those who may prefer it there is an "E" tuning fork that can be used instead of the "A" fork. The "E" fork is the sound or pitch of the open 1st string.

LESSON NUMBER TWO

Tuning the Second or "B" String

In order to tune the second string place any finger of the left hand on the 5th fret of this string. This note, at the 5th fret is the same "E" note as the open 1st string.

Below is a chart or diagram of the two identical "E" notes, and the Guitar notation of the identical "E" sound on the music staff.

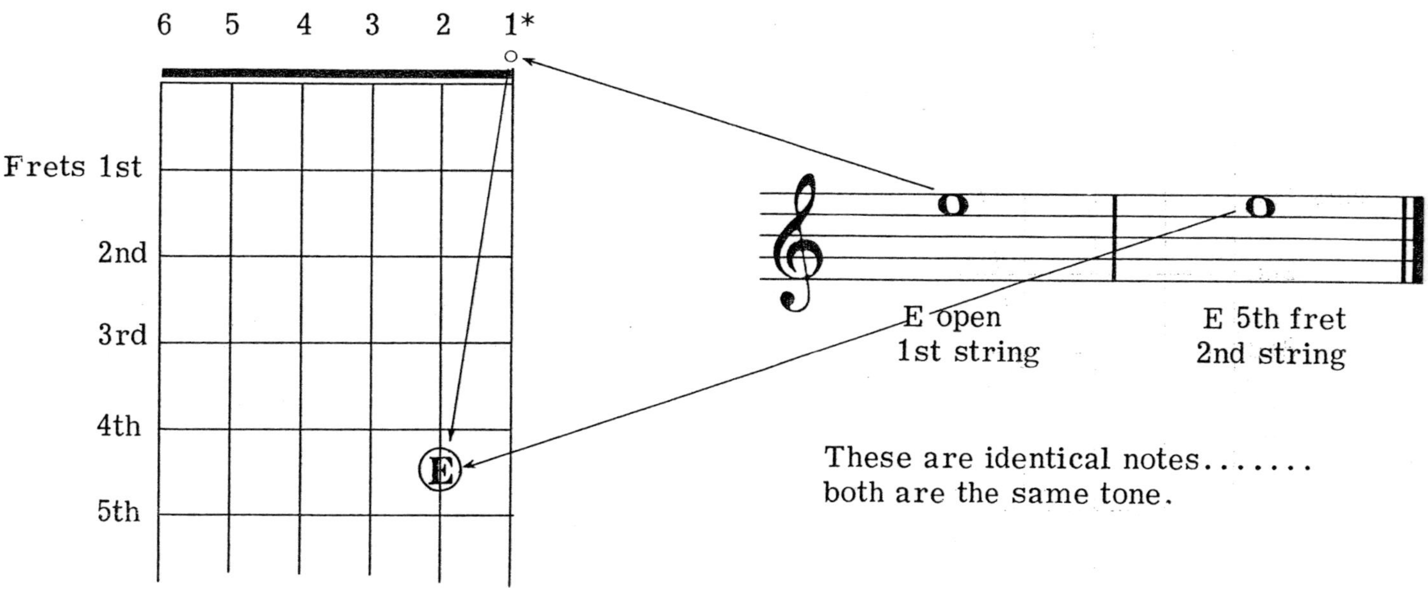

* The reference string

The first step towards tuning the second string is to LOOSEN it, thereby making it necessary to tighten it in order for the 5th fret tone to match the open 1st string. This process is called "raising the pitch". Work slowly, checking the two tones frequently. When you feel that you are "close" strike the two strings simultaneously,......the open 1st string and the 2nd string on the 5th fret. When you <u>are</u> in <u>tune</u>, the two strings will blend together as one tone, without discord or conflict.

Practice tuning the first and second strings many times before proceeding to the 3rd string. Accept the fact and convince yourself that this is a slow process and it will be some time before you can come up with a perfect tuning job. You get better with time and practice, and if you can accept this idea it will spare you a lot of disappointment and frustration. Some days will be better than others. The more you tune the more you improve.

LESSON NUMBER THREE

Tuning the Third or "G" String

In order to tune the 3rd string place a finger of the left hand at the 4th fret of this string. This note, at the 4th fret is the same "B" note as the open 2nd string.

Below is a chart or diagram of the two identical "B" notes showing the Guitar notation of the identical "B" sound on the music staff.

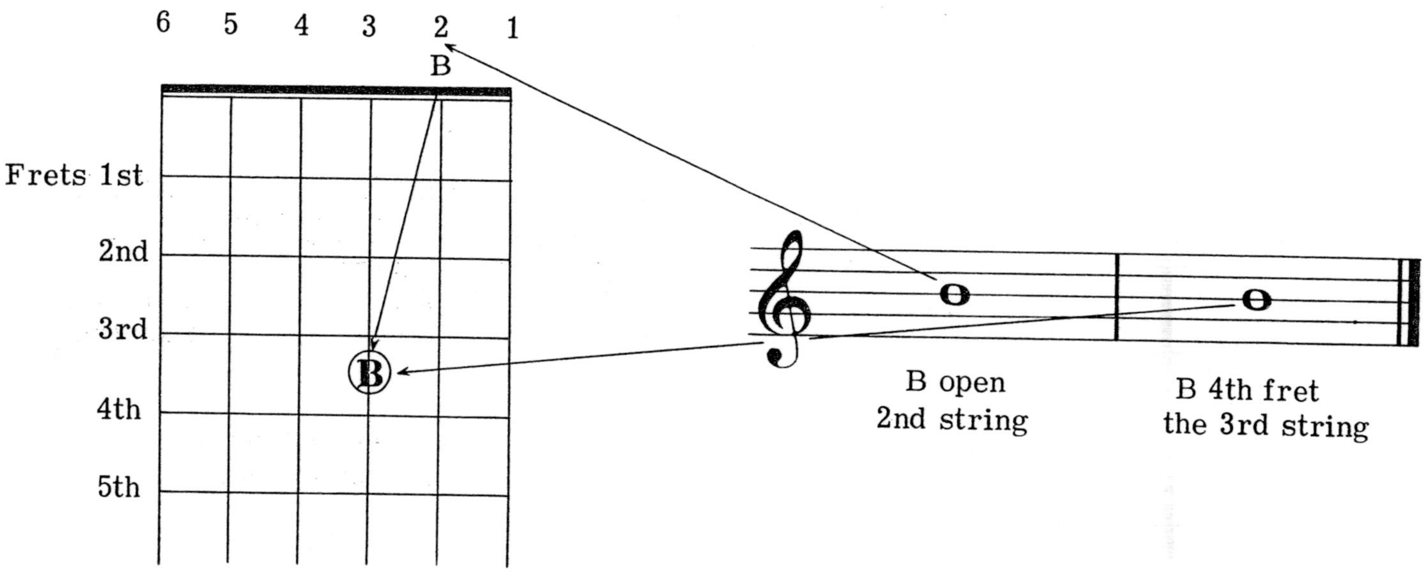

Continue the same procedure as in the previous lessons. Loosen the string you are tuning. It now becomes necessary to tighten it in order for the 4th fret tone to match the sound of the open 2nd string. As in the preceding lessons, work slowly, checking the two tones often. Frequently, when learning to tune, you may tighten the string too much and go higher in pitch than necessary. If you are in doubt as to whether or not you're too high, don't risk breaking a string, so, just loosen the string and start all over again. If you are taking lessons your instructor will guide you properly.

At this stage you should be reviewing the two previous lessons and satisfy yourself that you are progressing well enough on the first three strings before proceeding to the next string.

LESSON NUMBER FOUR

Tuning the Fourth or "D" String

To tune the 4th string, place a finger of the left hand on the 5th fret of this string. This note, at the 5th fret is the same "G" note as the open 3rd string.

Below is a chart or diagram of the two identical "G" notes showing the Guitar notation of the identical "G" sound on the music staff.

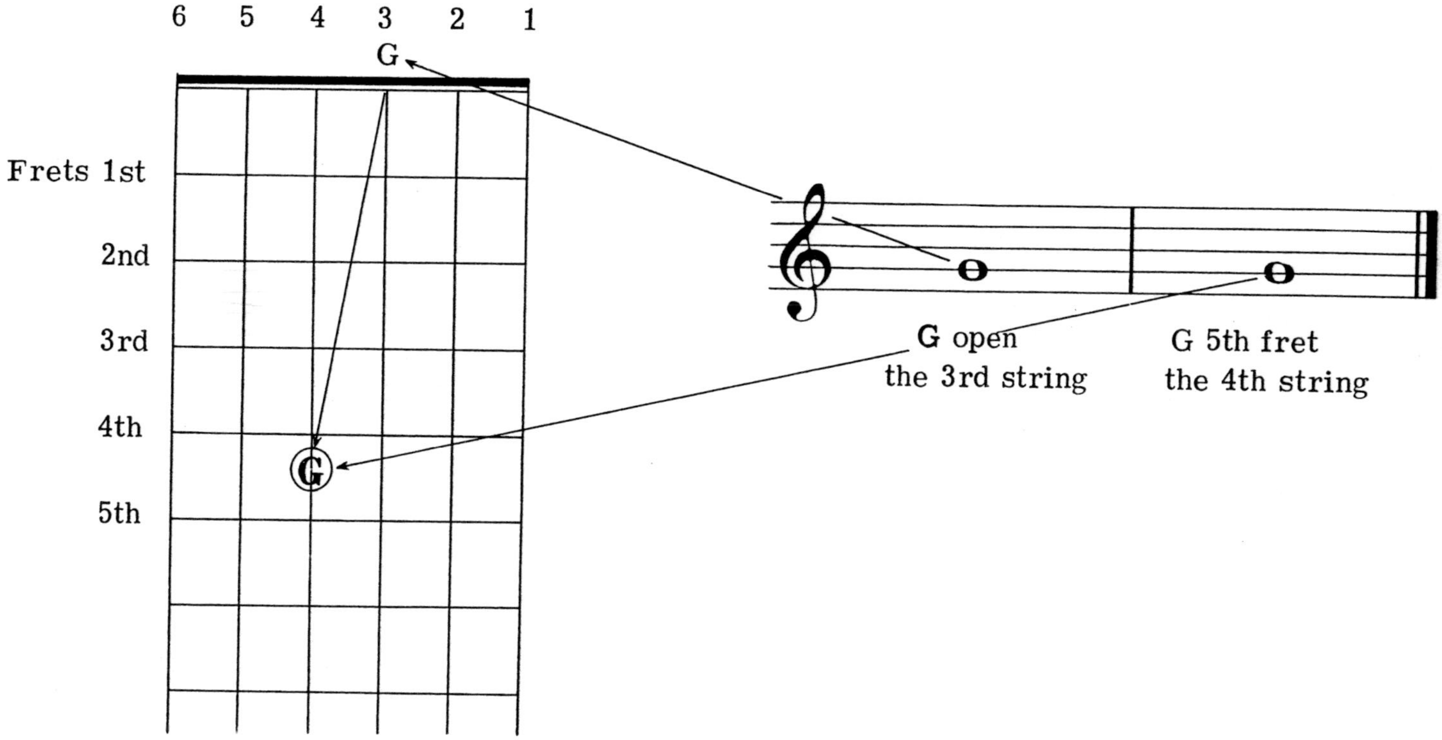

Continue in the same manner as in the preceding lessons. LOOSEN this string (the 4th) so that it will be necessary to tighten it in order for the 5th fret tone to match the sound of the open 3rd string. Practice self discipline and stick to fundamentals.

By now your ear will be developing to a greater degree, thus making it much easier to recognize the identical sounds.

LESSON NUMBER FIVE

Tuning the "A" or 5th String

To tune the 5th string, place a finger of the left hand on the 5th fret of this string. This note, at the 5th fret is the same "D" note as the open 4th string.

Below is a chart or diagram of the two identical "D" notes showing the guitar notation of the identical "D" sound on the music staff.

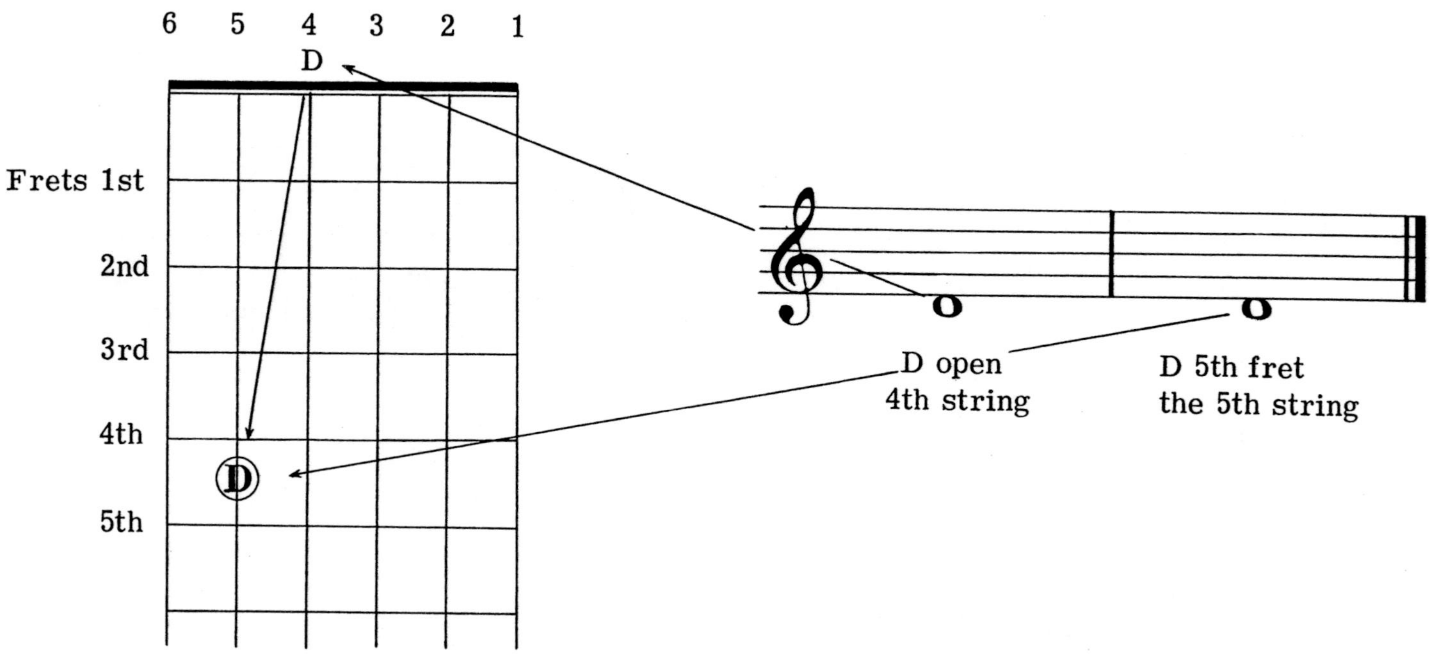

Rules are the same as in the preceding lessons.
Re-capping the important points........

1. Loosen string (5th) you are about to tune.
2. Press it down at the 5th fret.
3. Tighten it so that the 5th fret tone will match the open "D" (4th string).
4. Tune slowly. Do not hurry.

LESSON NUMBER SIX

Tuning the "E" or Sixth String

To tune the 6th string, place a finger of the left hand at the 5th fret of this string.

This note, at the 5th fret is the same "A" note as the open 5th string.

Below is a chart or diagram of the two identical "A" notes showing the Guitar notation of the identical "A" sound on the music staff.

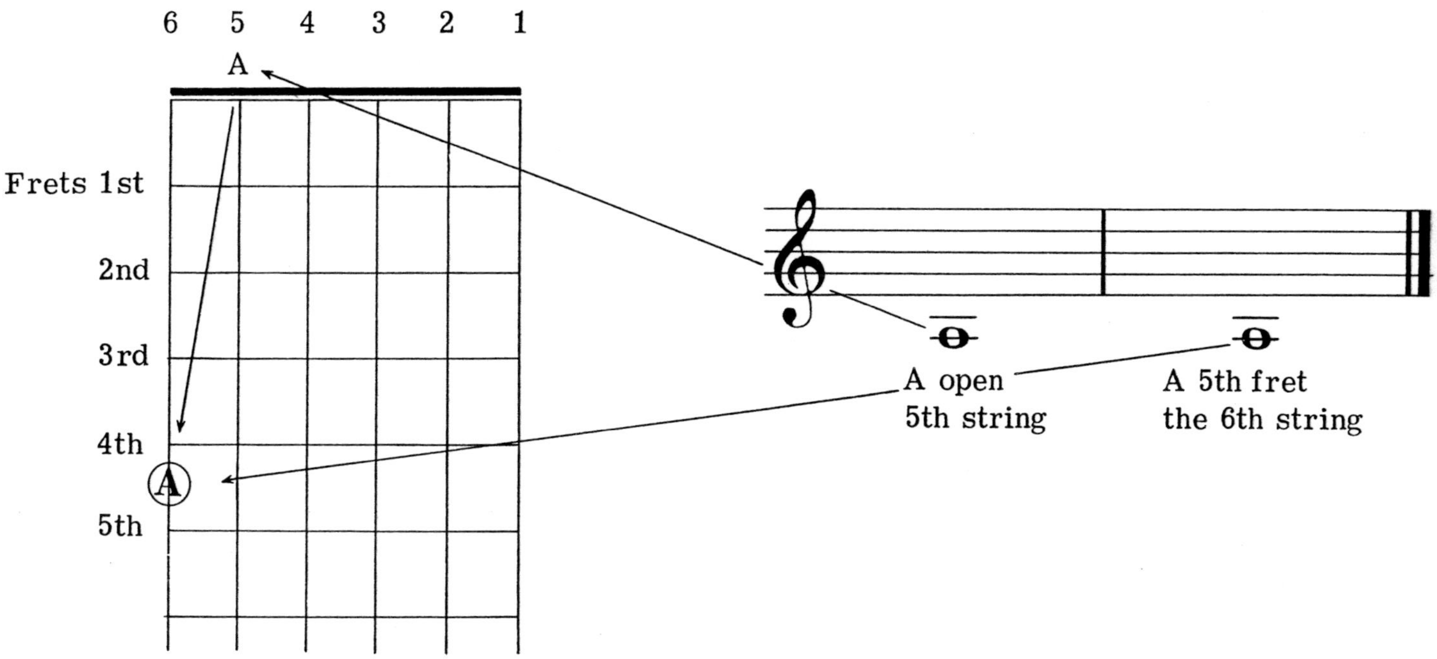

Rules and procedures are obviously unnecessary at this point. This lesson completes Phase Two of "How to tune your Guitar". Remember, you can only learn to tune by "tuning" the guitar. There is no magic or short cut to learning. It is all the result of hard work and application. The next pages will be devoted to further steps you can take to be able to tune like a "professional".

CHECKING UP ON YOUR TUNING

Upon completion of the tuning cycle, System One or System Two, check yourself to see how well you have done. There are a number of ways you may experiment with. Listed below are a few of the ways that have produced excellent results.

Play a few measures of any standard well known tune in accompaniment style. Preferably a simple tune with only two or three chord changes. For example:

SKIP TO MY LOU

Experiment further with other combinations of chords such as C, F and G7.... G, C and D7.... D, G and A7. This will help considerably in determining if you are in tune.

If the above tip has not turned the "trick" then try playing all of the natural notes you have learned beginning with the open "E" or 6th string and ending with the high "A" at the 5th fret of the 1st string:

The Scale of Natural Notes

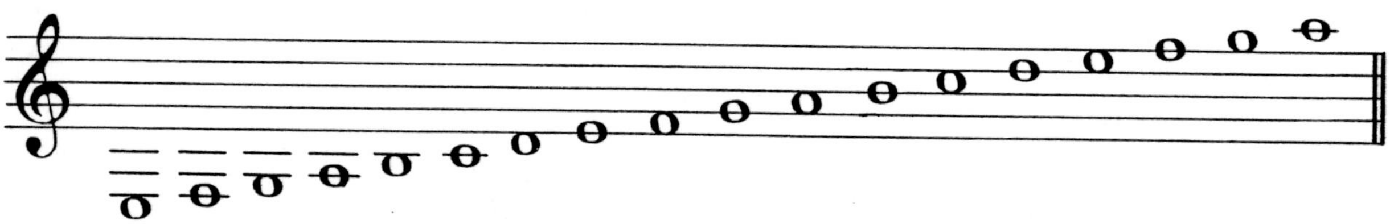

or, --- you can try four measures of "Yankee Doodle"

On the next page we will introduce an Identical Note chart. This is the first step towards acquiring the important "know how" leading up to precision tuning.

IDENTICAL NOTE CHART

An Important Study Leading Up to Precision Tuning

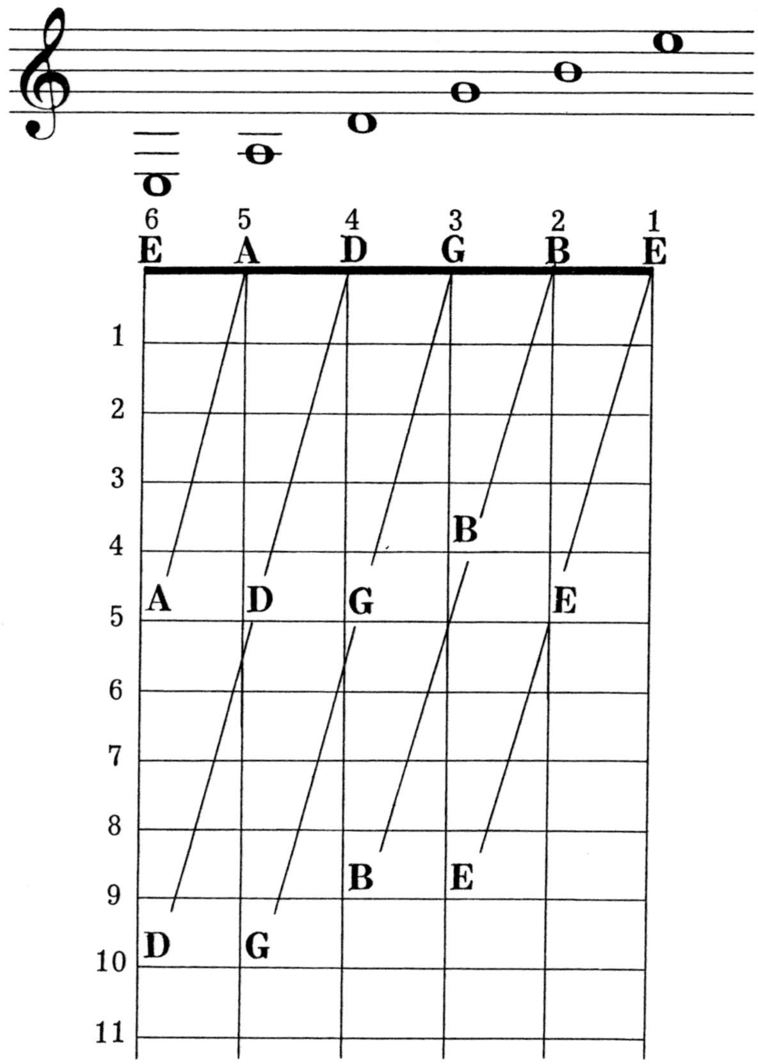

E - open 1st string, E - 5th fret 2nd string and E - 9th fret 3rd string are identical
B - open 2nd string, B - 4th fret 3rd string and B - 9th fret 4th string are identical
G - open 3rd string, G - 5th fret 4th string and G -10th fret 5th string are identical
D - open 4th string, D - 5th fret 5th string and D -10th fret 6th string are identical
A - open 5th string, A - 5th fret 6th string are identical.

The identical notes of each open string will have the same "pitch" or tone. However, the closed strings will have a different quality of sound, or timbre. Closed strings will not sound as brilliant as the open string and it is important that the student recognize this discrepancy in the sound.

When the open string and it's identical note have the same pitch you are in tune.

The next page will be devoted to a study of identical notes. Observe string markings faithfully.

Practice Page of Identical Notes
Observe String Markings

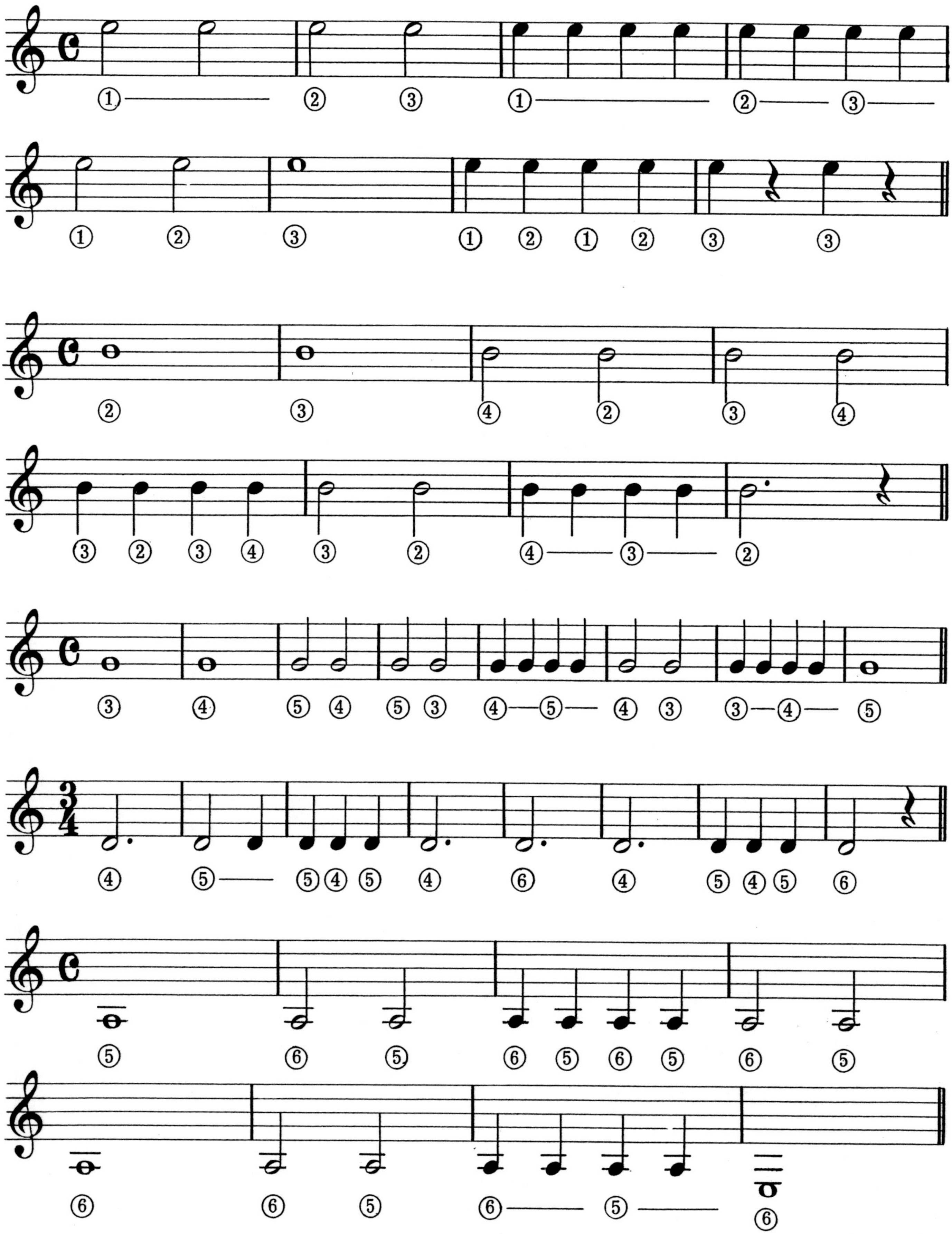

PIN-POINT TUNING THROUGH THE USE OF IDENTICAL NOTES

Tune the first three strings to "E" as shown in the charts below. When this is done, your first, second and third strings will be in perfect tune.

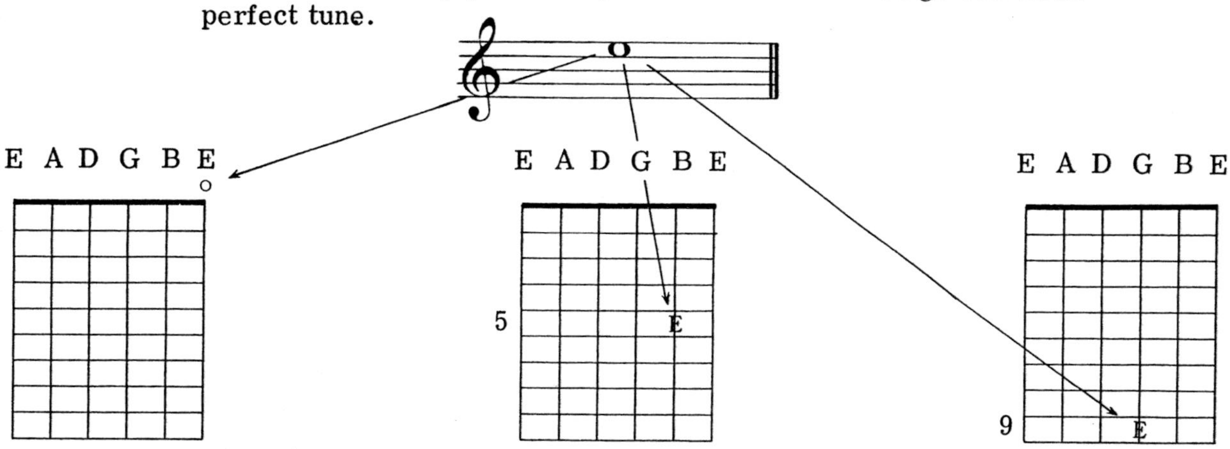

The second step is to tune the 4th and 5th strings to "G" as shown in the charts below. When this step is completed, the 4th and 5th strings will be in tune.

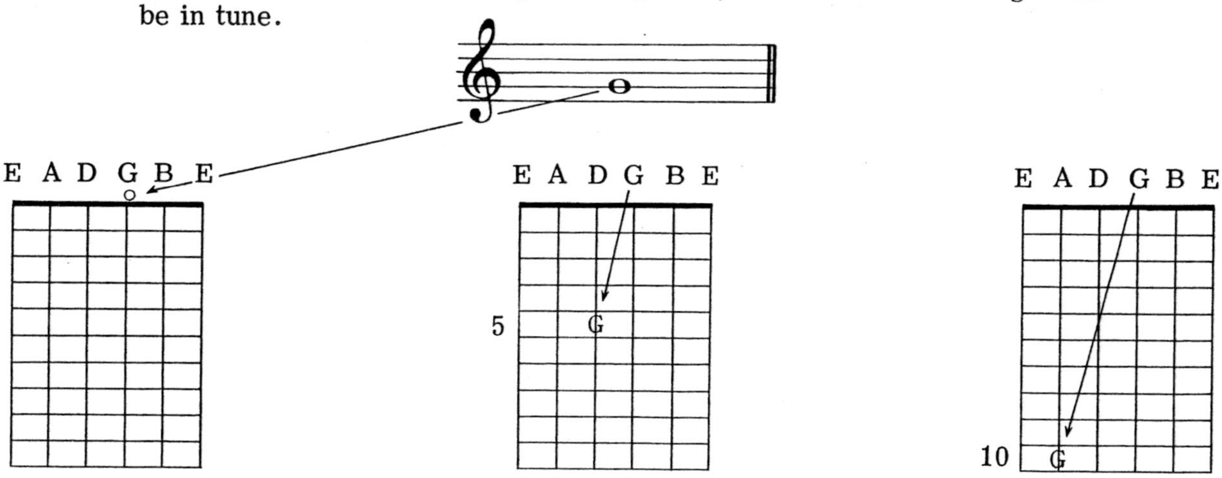

The final step is to tune the 5th and 6th strings to "D" as shown in the charts below. With the completion of this final step ALL strings will be in perfect tune. Go over the entire "cycle" a second time for insurance.

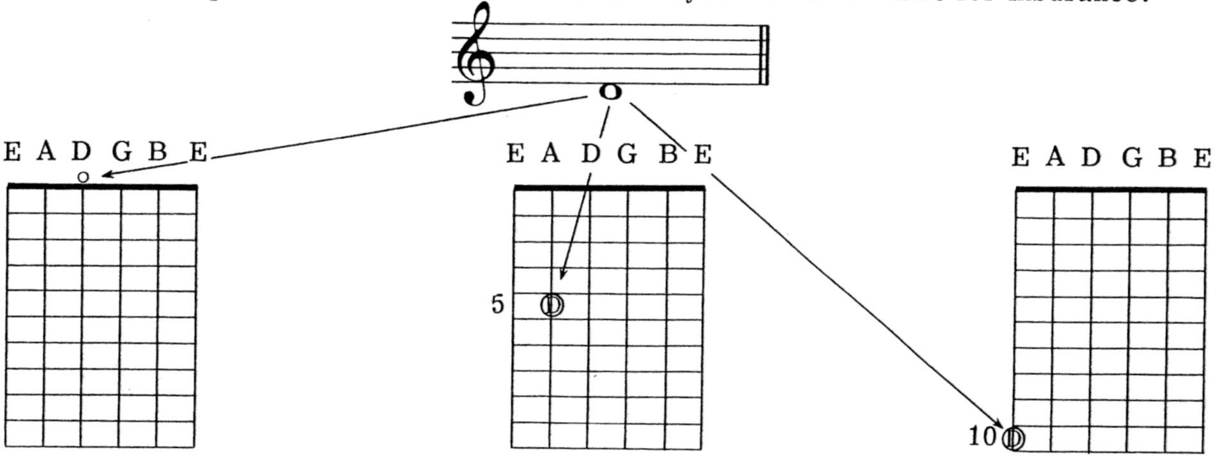

ACCURACY CHECK THE HARMONIC WAY

We do not recommend the Harmonic way as a basic method of tuning. Harmonics should be used only after you have learned to tune the guitar in your favorite manner, and then, only to test accuracy. This is NOT for the beginner.

Below are separate charts showing identical harmonics in each of the charts.
Tune the higher string to the lower string.

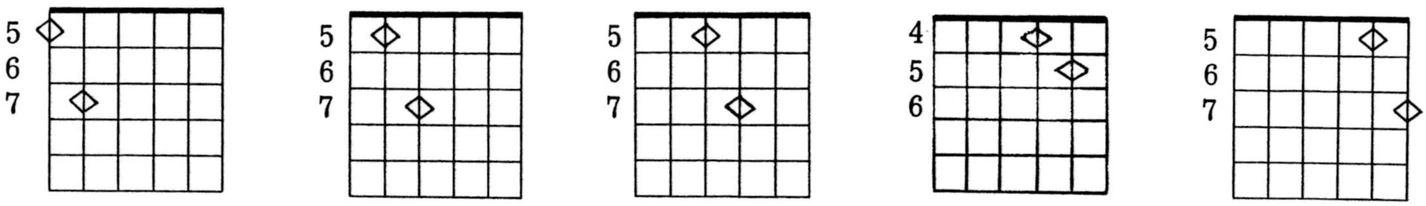

There is one big advantage in tuning the harmonic way. It leaves your left hand free to tune after striking the harmonics.

ACCURACY CHECK

Octave Tuning

Obviously there are still many ways to check for "Accuracy". However, we have covered the fundamental ways and will close with this last chapter covering "Octaves". We will use the "C" major chord in the 1st position. Hold the "C" chord and check it out as recommended below.

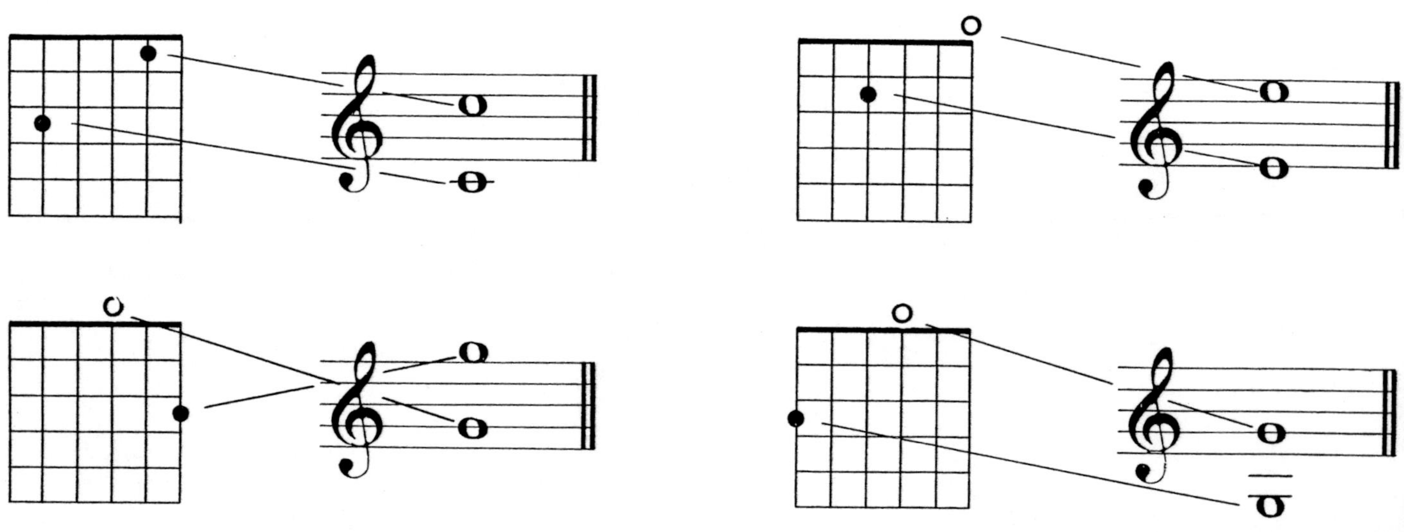